For

D1384299

~Best~
Friends

By Claudine Gandolfi

Illustrated by Richard Judson Zolan

Peter Pauper Press, Inc.
White Plains, New York

To the best friends anyone could wish for.
We've laughed, we've cried, then we've
laughed at what we cried about.
You know who you are.

∾

Artist: Richard Judson Zolan
Illustrations copyright ©1998
Art Licensing Properties, LLC.

Book design by Mullen & Katz

Introduction

One of the most precious gifts you can give yourself is a best friend. You'll know her by the way she helps you through rough times, always keeps an open mind, and enhances enjoyment of the good times. She can tell how you're feeling with just a glance or by the tone of your voice. She'll give you wings to fly and a hand to fall back on.

Let her know just how much you appreciate her. Give her a call, a visit, or a hug. If you're searching for just the right thing to say, the following pages may offer some inspiration.

C. G.

*L*ife is a symphony and
friendship is its theme.

~

*B*e the best friend you can be and
you'll have the best friends that
you could ever want.

Best Friends

Lend an ear to someone who needs it.
In return, not only will you receive
a shoulder to cry on but a friend
to share good times with.

~

A best friend is the sister
that destiny forgot to give you.

*W*hen you can
both laugh at
past indiscretions,
you know you share an
unbreakable bond.

A best friend will
congratulate you on a job well done and
console you when you need it.

❦

*Y*our best friend,
like your conscience, will always guide
you to the right decision.

Best Friends

Old friends are like your favorite
sweater—sensible, warm, and forgiving.

∽

Distance and time
cannot alter a friendship.

Best Friends

Like classic works of art, once
thought lost, friendships become more
dear when rediscovered.

Take the time to contact an old friend;
you'll be surprised at how quickly
you return to your old banter.